THE
EVACUATION
OF
SICK
AND
WOUNDED
FROM
MOBILE
COLUMNS

THE EVACUATION OF SICK AND WOUNDED FROM MOBILE COLUMNS

A. H. MACKLIN, O.B.E. M.C. M.D. [Vict.]
Late Major R.A.M.C., Senior Medical Officer to the Mobile Columns, North Russian Syren Expeditionary Force.

The Naval & Military Press Ltd

Published by
The Naval & Military Press Ltd
5 Riverside, Brambleside, Bellbrook
Industrial Estate, Uckfield, East Sussex,
TN22 1QQ England

Tel: +44 (0) 1825 749494
Fax: +44 (0) 1825 765701

www.naval-military-press.com
www.military-genealogy.com

In reprinting in facsimile from the original, any imperfections are inevitably reproduced and the quality may fall short of modern type and cartographic standards.

CHAPTER I.   THE MOBILE COLUMNS.

CHAPTER II.   CONDITIONS IN THE AREA OF OPERATIONS.

CHAPTER III.   MODES OF TRAVEL IN SNOWBOUND COUNTRIES.—TRANSPORT.

CHAPTER IV.   MEDICAL REQUIREMENTS.

CHAPTER V.   GENERAL SCHEME OF EVACUATION.

CHAPTER VI.   ORGANISATION.

CHAPTER VII.   EQUIPMENT.

CHAPTER VIII. SOME SPECIAL ARTICLES OF EQUIPMENT.

CHAPTER IX.   FROST-BITE.

CHAPTER X.   CONCLUSION.
               APPENDICES.

ILLUSTRATIONS.*

1.—A Reindeer Convoy passing along the surface of a frozen river.
2.—A Horse Ambulance Sledge.
3.—The Collection of Wounded by Dog Transport.
4.—The Special Sleeping Bag for Wounded.
5.—Ditto.
6.—A Medical Tent.
7.—The Shackleton Pattern Boots.

MAP.

The Area occupied during the Winter by the Syren Force.

DIAGRAM.

To illustrate "Casualties in the Fighting Area."

* The artist's drawings are by Miss Dorothy Travers-Pope.

FOREWORD.

During the Autumn of 1918 it became apparent to the Higher Command of the " Syren " North Russian Expeditionary Force that ordinary arrangements for the Evacuation of Sick and Wounded would not be satisfactory for the peculiar conditions of the Area occupied.

Instructions were therefore issued to the Assistant Director of Medical Services, as head of that Service in the Country, to arrange for the organisation and equipping of an efficient service.

This in turn was entrusted to me by the A.D.M.S.

In the carrying out of this duty it quickly became apparent that there would be many difficulties, the most serious of which are here enumerated:

1. Whereas in dealing with the Evacuation of Wounded in areas where communication was less difficult than in North Russia, the equipment was designed to be light and easily transportable, nevertheless the weight and bulk, as laid down in the establishments for that purpose, was too great for travel in snow-bound regions.
2. Whereas in temperate climates wounded men may survive two or three days of " lying out," untreated and exposed to the elements, this was not possible in the low temperature of the Arctic.
3. That with all sick or wounded men who were unable to walk, and so by muscular effort maintain an active circulation of the blood, and especially those who might be suffering from shock or collapse, frost-bite was liable to supervene.
4. No record could be found where sick and wounded had been dealt with under similar conditions, and there was, therefore, no guiding precedent.

Consequently it was necessary to evolve from first principles a scheme that would enable sick and wounded men to survive.

As the arrangements began to evolve and become more clear, I saw that success would depend almost entirely on transport and equipment, and that actual medical and surgical treatment, though not actually diminishing in importance, would be relatively less important.

Scales of equipment were drawn up. When put to the test I discovered that the weight that could be safely transported was very small, and that every article that could possibly be done without must be rigidly eliminated. To ensure success those articles which were retained had to be efficient.

The work done was as follows: First of all, before the first fall of snow, I travelled extensively in the country, noting conditions of surface, quantity and nature of trees abounding, presence or absence of villages, and presence or absence in these villages of material which could be adapted to medical requirements. The Russian, Karelian, and Lapp inhabitants were studied, and points noted with regard to their future usefulness.

When snow fell I again travelled extensively, noting and testing the different forms of transport in use in the different parts of the country.

This done, I returned to the Base and drew up my scheme and establishments as shown in the thesis.

It is possible that these papers may be criticised as dealing with a subject not sufficiently closely allied to the Science of Medicine. I would suggest, however (especially since the Great War), that " Evacuation of Sick and Wounded " is a branch of the Great Mother Stem of Medicine in its wide sense, requiring careful administration and careful carrying out, and upon the success or failure of which depends largely the making or marring of the very best of British men.

This work is carried out entirely by fully qualified medical men, both of the Royal Army Medical Corps, and civilian practitioners, temporarily commissioned, and in its performance many have lost their lives.

Moreover, I submit that, in the depth of the Russian forest, a box of matches is of more value for the saving of life than many highly elaborate and more technical appliances.

In laying this thesis before the examiners it has been my object, although the subject is of an essentially military nature, to avoid military phraseology and technical terms. To eradicate them entirely has not been possible.

I have tried to present it as the solution not so much of a military problem as of a medical problem.

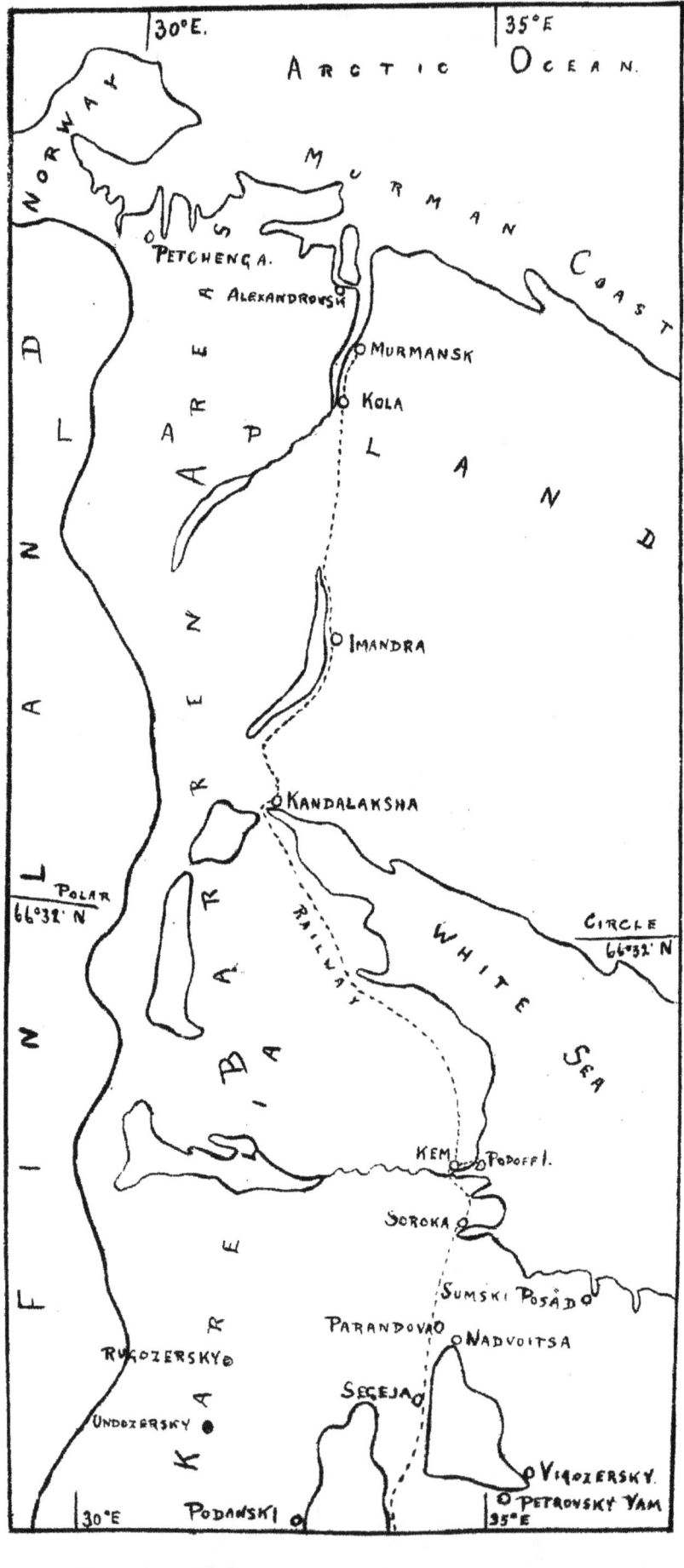

CHAPTER I.

THE MOBILE COLUMNS.

The area occupied by the North Russia " Syren " Expeditionary Force during the winter of 1918-19 extended from latitude 62° North to lattitude 70° North, and from longitude 29° East to longitude 35° East. The country was composed of dense forest, interspersed with rivers, lakes, and large swamps, and was deeply covered with snow.

The population was extremely scanty and composed of three different races: Russian, Karelian, and Lapp.

The Russians occupied Petchenga, on the Murman Coast, Murmansk (the railway terminus), Kola, Kandalaksha, Kem, and Soroka, situated on the railway line; scattered villages in the south of the area, and along the White Sea coast.

The Karelians occupied scattered villages in the area contiguous to the Finnish border.

The Lapps, a nomadic race, occupied the area known as Russian Lapland, the part of this area situated north of Kandalaksha. They had no permanent settlements.

The only good line of communication consisted of the Petrograd-Murmansk Railway, running in a North and South direction parallel to the Finnish border.

One reindeer sledge track used by the Lapps connected Petchenga with Kola, and some pony sledge tracks linked the villages in the more populous southern portion of the area. There were no good roads.

The climate was cold, but the temperature was very variable, due to the influence of the Gulf Stream, which sends a warm current along the edge of the Murman Coast, keeping it entirely free from ice. The snow surface consequently varied, being sometimes dry, sometimes slushy and wet, but the country remained snowbound all the winter.

Military operations in the " Syren " Force previous to the signing of the Armistice, were directed to the defence of the ice-free ports on the Murman Coast, and of the railway line. Finland was occupied by the Germans, and the Allied front, roughly speaking, was the Finnish Border. The main line of communication in this case ran parallel to the " front line."

After the signing of the Armistice and the withdrawal of the Germans from Finland, which was left by them in a destitute condition, operations were directed against the Bolshevists in the South.

The situation can be understood by reference to the accompanying map.

Ordinary equipment and means of transport proved quite inadequate for use in this area, and so units known as "The Mobile Columns" were formed to carry out operations against the enemy.

Each Mobile Column was a unit complete in itself, organised and equipped so as to be able to move rapidly over the snow, absolutely self-contained, and independent of outside supplies for a definite period.

The Mobile Column was therefore, broadly speaking, a unit designed to go from a centre over barren, trackless, snowbound regions, attack the enemy, and return. During the time it was absent it had to depend entirely on its own resources, and had to carry all its own cover, food, and fodder for animals.

The main points in connection with each Mobile Column are as follows:—

1. Total number of personnel employed, 262.
2. Maximum time absent during operations, 15 days; and maximum distance covered, 200 miles.
3. Wheeled transport and pack animals could not be used, and sledges were the only means of conveyance possible.
4. Transport consisted of sledges drawn by horses, reindeer, dogs, or men.
5. The weight and bulk of equipment was rigidly limited, and permitted the carrying of no extras.
6. The climate was extremely cold, and required special measures for protection against it.
7. 262 men proceeding in column of route through snow leave a well-marked trail, and so a column was always connected to its centre by a "made trail," which permitted of much faster travel than unbroken country.
8. Although each Mobile Column was equipped to be self-dependent, full advantage would be taken of all local facilities.
9. All ranks were trained in the use of skis and snowshoes.
10. Cases of sick and wounded were liable to occur at any time.

CHAPTER II.

CONDITIONS IN AREA OF OPERATIONS.

In the preparation of a medical service to deal with wounded of the Mobile Columns, I first made a study of the conditions in the Area of Operations. Extensive journeys were made into the area, and the results of my observations are as follows:—

The conditions under which Mobile Columns might operate for any one plan of operation varied greatly, and may be classified under the following headings:—

1. Varieties of Snow Surface.
2. Populated Areas.
3. Barren Areas.
4. Combination of 2 and 3.
5. Types of Transport available.

This classification does not include differences in conditions due to strategical plans, but refers to the area only.

1. VARIETIES OF SNOW SURFACE.

Snow varies greatly in its characteristics, depending chiefly on the temperature and presence or not of winds. As many varieties of surface may be found in a snowbound country as in one enjoying a temperate climate. Just as in one case one finds surfaces varying from good, hard roads to ploughed fields, so in the other one finds an equal number of variations in surface. Moreover, just as the transport which is possible on the different surfaces of a temperate climate varies, so also does the type of transport necessary for each variety of surface vary in snowbound regions.

Snow surfaces may be classified as follows: —

(a) HARD TRACKS. These are formed by constant usage, and present a hard, shiny, slippery surface, offering little resistance to sledge-runners. They are best in extreme cold, and become slightly soft and sticky with a rise of temperature. Recent falls of snow also render the surface soft and sticky to sledge-runners.

(b) POOR TRACKS. These may have been formed by constant usage but afterwards abandoned, or by infrequent usage. They usually present a hard under-surface, but are covered with varying depths of snow, and may in places be heavily drifted up.

(c) UNBROKEN COUNTRY presents many varieties: (i) Frozen rivers present a surface similar to those described in poor tracks. The travelling surface varies with the depth of snow which has fallen on them. In places the ice may not be frozen, e.g., rapids; in other places deep snow drifts may have formed. (ii) Frozen lakes resemble frozen rivers, but if of large extent they may be exposed to strong winds (i.e., they lose the protective influence of trees). Winds have the effect of blowing away loose surface snow and massing it in drifts against obstacles such as banks, trees, etc., and of packing the remainder, giving a good travelling surface, especially in extreme cold. (iii) TUNDRA is composed of exposed areas, which in summer are very swampy, composed of marsh, interspersed with numerous tussocks and hummocks. They present an extremely bad travelling surface when snow-covered. (iv) WOODED AND TIMBERED COUNTRY. Owing to the shelter afforded by trees, the snow packs very loosely. This type of country presents an extremely bad travelling surface, often complicated by fallen branches, stumps and roots of trees, and by outcrops of hard rock. (v) SEA ICE. This presents a great variety of surfaces. Being exposed to strong winds, the snow packs tightly, but sastrugi, or wind ridges, are liable to form, making an irregular surface. Tidal movements and strong winds may cause the ice to break up and mass together, forming hummocks and pressure ridges very difficult to negotiate.

2. POPULATED AREAS.

In areas where villages are situated within a day's journey of each other the conditions differ largely from those met with in barren areas. "The Englishman's home is his castle," but this is not the case with the peasants of Northern Russia, where it is the usual thing for travellers to enter any house they fancy and accommodate themselves for the night, making use of any facilities which the house offers in the way of stoves, cooking utensils, and beds.*

Every Russian householder owned a pony and sledge, which were necessary for the existence of himself and his family, and the villages were connected up by well-formed, constantly-used, hard tracks.

Consequently, from the point of view of the evacuation of Sick and Wounded, each village formed a ready-made "relay post" (vide infra), providing both housing accommodation and transport.

Where these conditions prevailed a certain amount of equipment, tents, cooking appliances, sledges and animal transport could be dispensed with.

* The A.D.M.S. adopted the wise policy of treating civilian sick. As they were destitute of medical assistance in any form, the "Krasnaya Krest" (Red Cross) was eagerly welcomed everywhere. They were very grateful for assistance received, which facilitated the obtaining of local supplies.

3. BARREN AREAS.

In areas composed of forest, tundra, frozen rivers and lakes, without villages or tracks, the conditions were very different from those met with in 2. In this case the Mobile Column would have to travel fully equipped in every way, carrying everything necessary for their needs.

The difficulty of travel is very much greater, primarily because of the unbroken country, and secondly because of the extra weight of equipment necessary.

4. COMBINATIONS OF 2 AND 3,

e.g., where the Column would operate partly in a populated area, leaving it to cross a barren area. In this case the weight and bulk of equipment could be decreased but not dispensed with to the extent as in 2.

5. TYPE OF TRANSPORT AVAILABLE.

This point will be dealt with more fully under "TRANSPORT." There were four main types of transport—reindeer, ponies, dogs, and men. Of these the reindeer were best for barren areas, but the area in which they could be used was limited to that in which reindeer moss grew. Ponies were most suitable for the populated areas. Dogs could be used under all conditions, and when ponies and reindeer would be useless. Men could also be used under all conditions; they were the most reliable form of haulage power, but slowest and most extravagant in food, and required the most elaborate sleeping accommodation.

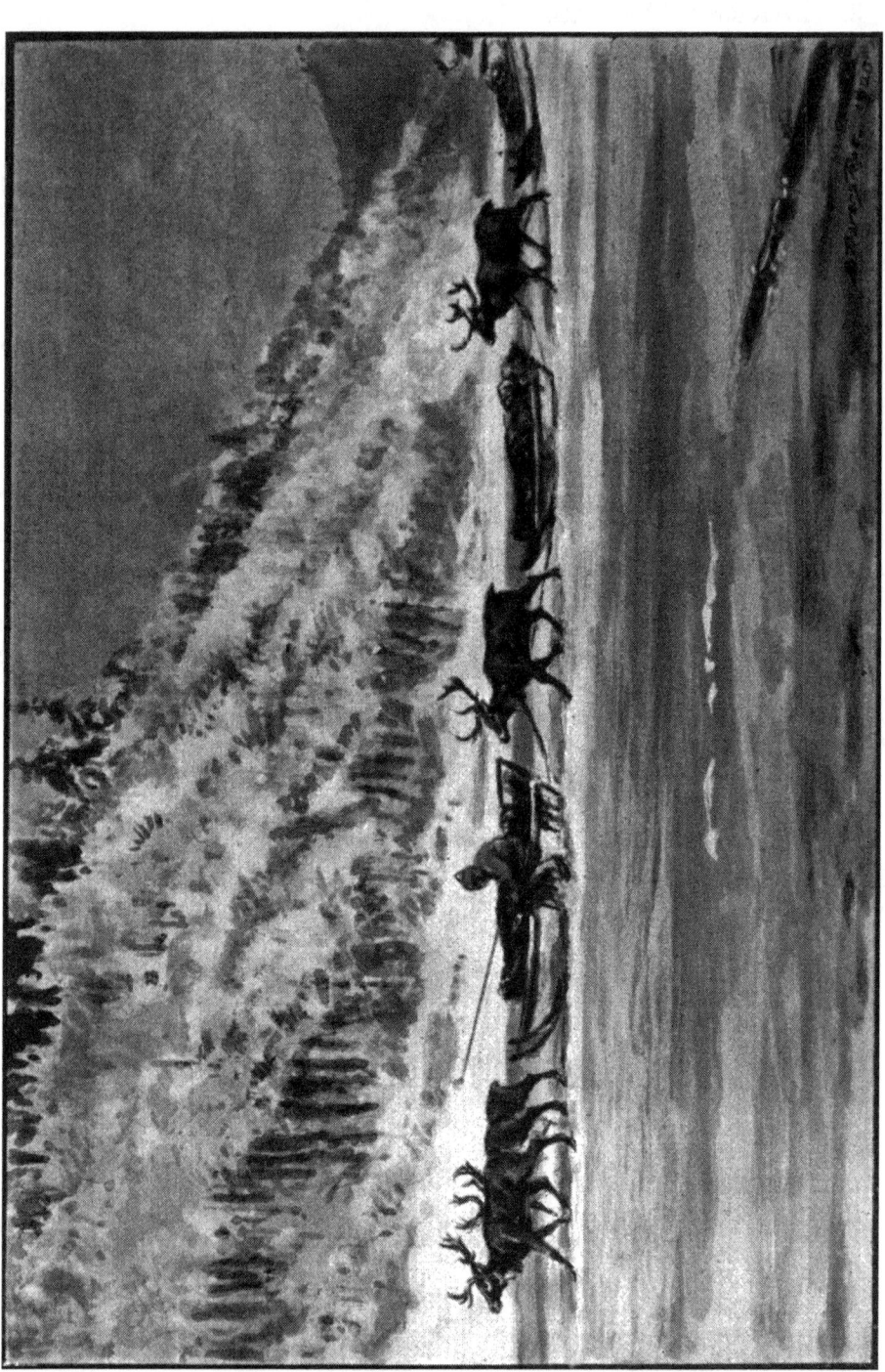

CHAPTER III.

MODES OF TRAVEL IN SNOWBOUND COUNTRIES.—TRANSPORT.

FOOT TRAVEL.

When snow has packed hard or presents a crust sufficiently thick to bear the weight of a man, it is possible to move about with only the footgear which is essential to warmth; but when it is soft and deep, or the crust is thin, the labour of walking, when the feet and legs sink to a depth of one to three feet, is so great that the distance which can be covered daily is almost negligible. To overcome this two forms of footgear are in common use: the ski and the snow-shoe. Skis, like boots, are made in pairs, and consist of long, thin, flat pieces of wood, which are attached to the boots, and enable one to travel considerably faster than on foot. They are most suitable when the snow has a crust, and permit of travel at an average speed of four miles per hour. Snow-shoes are particularly suitable for deep, soft snow, but progress in them is comparatively slow.

SLEDGES.

The only form of vehicle possible is one which proceeds on runners, wheels being quite useless. Sledges vary in size, shape, and weight, and with the different kinds of animal used for drawing them.

In the area of operation four modes of transport were available:—
1. Reindeer; 2. Ponies; 3. Dogs; 4. Men.

REINDEER TRANSPORT.

In order to investigate the suitability of reindeer transport for Sick and Wounded, I made a journey of 120 miles into Lapland, travelling all the time by reindeer sledge, and made the following observations:—

(1) Each reindeer can pull a weight of 250 lbs. 30 to 40 miles daily for several days, but then requires a prolonged rest.

(2) Their use is limited to areas in which reindeer moss grows in sufficient quantities and sufficiently widely spread to enable them to be taken to a feeding ground at the end of each day's journey.

(3) No fodder or cover need be carried on the journey; it is only necessary to take them to a moss-bed each night, and there leave them until morning, with the one precaution of tying them together to prevent them being stampeded by wolves.

(4) They are capable of negotiating all kinds of surface, and of climbing and descending with safety steep gradients and river banks.

(5) The pull on the sledges is very smooth and regular.

(6) Lapp drivers are essential for satisfactory work. They do not require any accommodation, are quite capable of looking after themselves at night, and require only their rations.

(7) The sledges used by the Lapps for reindeer are of two types:—
- (1) A high raised sledge on runners, suitable for carrying Sick and Wounded, but would require that the pace be reduced to dead slow on gradients and over rough country to prevent sledges capsizing. Also it would be advisable to have one attendant to, at most, every two of these sledges.
- (2) A smaller sledge shaped like a boat, with rounded bottom. An excellent all-purposes sledge, and in it sick or lightly wounded cases could be comfortably carried. Equipment can be easily stored in them and tightly lashed, after which it requires no attention. Owing to their rounded shape they roll badly in rough country, but cannot capsize.

(8) One Lapp driver can manage any number of sledges in convoy up to twelve, the method adopted being as follows:—

The driver occupies the front or driving sledge, to which is attached three reindeer. The remaining reindeer and sledges follow in single file, each reindeer being attached to the sledge in front.

One reindeer with a jangling bell is attached to and runs behind the last sledge, the jangling of the bell serving to notify the driver in front that the convoy is intact.

I tested pony transport over the same type of country and found that ponies could accomplish neither the speed nor the daily distance, and required that fodder should be carried. I also discovered that some of the gradients and steep banks negotiated by the reindeer were impossible for ponies.

I had (whilst serving as a dog driver on the Imperial Trans-Antarctic Expedition) considerable experience of dogs. That they could negotiate the country I had no doubt, but they could not accomplish the speed or daily distance, and required that food should be carried. I considered them inferior to reindeer for the purpose.

Looked at from all points of view, I considered reindeer transport satisfactory and decided to use it wherever the conditions of the area permitted.

An establishment was consequently drawn up, vide Appendix.

PONY TRANSPORT.

To investigate this I made a journey of over 400 miles in the more populous areas by pony sledge, passing from village to village, and examining the accommodation in each with regard to Relay Posts. On the return journey I placed myself in the position of a wounded man lying in the sledge, protected from the cold by a sleeping-bag of the type decided upon for wounded. In this case I did not stop at the villages, but, waiting only to secure fresh animals, passed rapidly on, travelling by day and night. The following observations were made:—

(1) A pony can pull two men with equipment, in addition to the driver, from 20 to 30 miles daily; in the case of emergency the daily distance can be increased to 40 miles, but this cannot be maintained indefinitely. Average speed four to five miles per hour.

(2) Local supplies of fodder cannot be relied upon and must be carried.

(3) This form of transport can only be used with advantage on hard tracks.

(4) They do not require house cover at night, a rug thrown over them is sufficient.

(5) Each pony requires a driver. The Russian owner of the pony generally prefers to drive himself, and this is the most satisfactory arrangement. He procures his own accommodation at night, and requires only his rations and fodder for the pony.

(6) The sledge used locally by Russians for their ponies is boat-shaped and set on runners. When packed with hay they make a comparatively warm and comfortable means of conveyance for Sick and Wounded, and will accommodate two lying cases. A hood can be fitted which gives protection against wind and driving snow.

(7) Over known tracks they travel equally well by day or night.

(8) They travel best when several proceed together in convoy. The best speed is obtained when the fastest pony is placed in front, each pony in the convoy striving not to be left behind. The ponies have a habit of placing their heads into the sledge in front in search of hay. This is a constant source of annoyance to sick and wounded men, and can be prevented by the use of the hood, or by a flag, or a branch of pine boughs secured to the back of the sledge.

In areas described previously as "populated areas" I considered this the best and a satisfactory mode of conveyance for sick and wounded, and an establishment (vide Appendix) was consequently drawn up.

DOG TRANSPORT.

The following observations are derived from experience gained as a dog driver for two years with the Shackleton Antarctic Expedition, and from journeys made with dogs supplied to the "Syren" Force, of which one team was allotted for my personal use:—

(1) Each dog can pull from 80 to 100 lbs., and more on occasion.

(2) They can negotiate every kind of surface, but for satisfactory work require that soft snow surfaces should be "broken" for them by a man preceding the sledge on snow shoes.

(3) The daily distance varies enormously with the type and condition of surface and varies from 5 to 30 miles daily.

(4) They require for hard work 2 lbs. of meat food daily.

(5) The sledges used for dogs vary; the best type is the Shackleton pattern Norwegian sledge, which is very strong and weighs less than 50 lbs. An Army pattern stretcher can be readily fitted to this and the patient secured so that he cannot fall off.

I placed great faith in the reliability of dogs, but as no local supplies were available, and as the dogs supplied to the Force were rather poor in condition, parasite infested, and ill-trained, I decided that both reindeer and pony transport were preferable each in its own area.

Nevertheless dog transport of wounded is a type which can be used at any time, dogs and dog-sledges are easily transportable by ship and railway. The dogs are extremely intelligent, and have great hardihood and adaptability. On the one occasion on which they were used for this purpose in Russia they rendered excellent service, and successfully penetrated an area impossible to other means of transport.

MAN HAULAGE.

Experience of this was gained during the Antarctic Expedition (vide supra) and observations were made with troops allotted for Mobile Column work.

(1) Each man should be able to pull his own weight.

(2) The average speed is two miles per hour on an average surface.

(3) Daily distance, five to fifteen miles.

(4) Men require more accommodation and food than other forms of transport.

(5) The slow rate of pulling allows sledge runners to stick, and consequently the work is harder than with faster transport, which keeps the sledges continually on the move and prevents sticking of the runners.

(6) It is necessary that the men be fit and interested in their work.

I determined from the above considerations only to use man-haulage in emergency, and in the field, where, owing to the noise of battle, animals would be unmanageable.

CHAPTER IV.

MEDICAL REQUIREMENTS.

To deal with the Sick and Wounded of the Mobile Columns, medical arrangements were necessary, and the medical requirements resolved themselves broadly into the problem of conveyance of Sick and Wounded a maximum distance of 100 miles over the snow, providing adequate protection against the cold during the journey.

At first sight the problem seemed to be very difficult, and it was thought that the chances of survival for a man, wounded, 100 miles distant from the nearest source of surgical assistance, were very remote.

The following general principles dealing with casualties were laid down, and the general scheme of evacuation moulded round them.

1. NECESSITY FOR ADEQUATE FIRST AID.

First Aid has the same value as in other regions, but must be rendered the more quickly in that cold rapidly benumbs and makes helpless a devitalised man. Each mobile unit should therefore have a large number of men trained in First Aid and capable of rendering assistance in emergency.

2. NECESSITY FOR PROVISION OF EARLY SKILLED ASSISTANCE AND CAREFUL PREPARATION FOR THE JOURNEY.

This is necessitated by the long route of evacuation, and the comparatively long time occupied in travelling before surgical treatment can be obtained. Every mobile unit should therefore be accompanied by a medical officer, whose Aid Post should be on, or as near, the field of operations as circumstances will permit, and as well equipped as possible taking into consideration the difficulty of transport. In the case, however, of the Column splitting into numerous small parties, the Aid Post must be in a central position, which may entail that it cannot be advanced to the scene of operations of any one party.

3. LIMITATION OF WEIGHT OF EQUIPMENT.

As large and complete equipment as possible is desirable, but it must be rigidly limited to a weight and bulk which can be safely transported and arrive at the scene of operations. Too great a weight necessarily means delay, and better a small equipment on the spot than one larger and more complete which, owing to its weight or bulk, has failed to arrive.

4. PREVENTION OF SHOCK AND COLLAPSE.

All injuries produce some degree of shock, and this is likely to be more severe when the patient is exposed to extreme cold. Collapse also is likely to supervene on the long and arduous route of evacuation, and therefore special attention must be paid to prevention of these conditions, and should be chiefly directed along the following lines:—

(a) Early and adequate treatment of the cause producing the shock (as per Paras. 1 and 2.)

(b) Artificial warmth. It is not sufficient merely to insulate the system against the cold outer air, for the circulation is depressed and body heat is lowered, and therefore some means of supplying artificial warmth must be provided.

5. RAPIDITY OF TRAVEL.

However well cared for and prepared at the Aid Post, a prolonged sledge journey in the extreme cold and over the rough tracks necessarily throws a strain on a badly wounded man, and the longer the journey the greater is likely to be the strain on his reserves. It is an established principle that wounded should be evacuated to the Casualty Clearing Station in the shortest possible time. The preparation of the patient at the Aid Post must be carefully carried out, but once started on the return journey the great principle should be "speed." When possible Relay Posts (see Para. 7) should be communicated with, so that the patient can be attended to at once, fresh transport prepared, and proceed with the least possible delay.

6. FIXED ROUTE OF EVACUATION.

Wherever possible, wounded should be evacuated over a "made" trail and a known route. It permits of faster and smoother travel, and the Relay System (see Para. 7) depends on it.

7. RELAY POSTS

should be established along the route of evacuation, and should be of two kinds:—

(a) MEDICAL RELAY POSTS, where the patient can be attended to, warmed, redressed if necessary, obtain hot food, and receive general attention.

(b) TRANSPORT RELAY POSTS, with fresh supplies of animals, so that tired animals can be exchanged for fresh and the patients be passed on without delay.

8. CONVOYS.

With all forms of animals used for drawing sledges the greatest speed is obtained when several travel together in convoy. It is only necessary to place the fastest animal, or group of animals, in front. This arrangement possesses other advantages—it is easier for the Relay Posts to deal with a large number at one time than with numerous single cases, and fewer guides and guards are necessary.

9. AN ADVANCED DRESSING STATION,

which may vary in form and size according to circumstances, should be arranged at the nearest possible point at which supplies can be obtained. This should always be arranged in conjunction with the M.O. i/c Mobile Column, who should be notified of its exact position, and no change should be made unless he can be notified with certainty of its new location.

CHAPTER V.

GENERAL SCHEME OF EVACUATION.

As already stated under "The Mobile Columns," broadly speaking the scheme of operation for each Mobile Column was as follows:—It proceeded from a centre, breaking a track through the snow till it reached within striking distance of its objective. At a selected point Camp was pitched. The troops then, in one or more parties, proceeded lightly equipped against the enemy. The objective might be a village, in which case, if the action were successful, it might be occupied. It was probable, however, that in most cases the Column would return over its own tracks, and the return journey—being over a broken trail—would be made in much shorter time than the outward journey.

The scheme of evacuation had to arrange for evacuation of:—

(1) Casualties in the battlefield from any one party or from all parties simultaneously.

(2) Stragglers on line of march.

I decided to organise (see Organisation) the System of Evacuation to follow as far as possible the already existing military procedure whereby a Regimental Medical Officer (to whom was attached a small number of R.A.M.C. personnel) accompanied the Unit, and was responsible for the evacuation of wounded from the battlefield to his Aid Post. From this point the responsibility devolved upon the Officer Commanding a Field Ambulance, whose duty it was to collect wounded from the Aid Post, and evacuate to a Dressing Station.

Thus in connection with each Mobile Column there would be 2 distinct Medical Units, one forming an integral part of the Mobile Column and accompanying it wherever it went, and another whose duty it was to keep in touch with the Regimental Medical Officer, working from behind over the trail made by the advancing column.

These two functioning bodies received the following names respectively:—

(1) The Mobile Column Medical Unit.
(2) The Relay System, composed of a number of small units.

(A) CASUALTIES ON THE BATTLEFIELD.

(1) FROM FIGHTING AREA TO AID POST.

The man when wounded to be attended on the spot by the Regimental Stretcher Bearers who render First Aid and evacuate him by sledge (man haulage or animal transport according to circumstances) to the Regimental Aid Post.

(2) AT AID POST.

Normally the M.O. to remain at his Aid Post, but his movements to vary with circumstances and be left to his discretion. The Aid Post to consist of a tent in Barren Areas, but whenever possible in populated areas of a commodious and well-warmed room. The wounded man to be examined, redressed, and prepared for the long sledge journey.

(3) FROM AID POST TO ADVANCED DRESSING STATION.

The wounded man to be collected and conveyed by ambulance sledge, the type to vary with the condition of the area of operations, to the Advanced Dressing Station (see General Principles), passing a series of Relay Posts (see General Principles). The sledge to be supplied with all equipment necessary to ensure his safe transit and protection from cold.

(4) AT A RELAY POST.

The Relay Post to be of 2 kinds, if possible contiguous.

(i) MEDICAL RELAY POST. Here the wounded and sick receive general attention, are given hot food, sanitary requirements attended to, and the wound, if necessary, redressed.

(ii) TRANSPORT RELAY POST, with fresh supply of animals, so that tired animals can be removed, fresh ones harnessed up, and the sledge proceed with the least possible delay.

(5) THE ADVANCED DRESSING STATION.

To be situated so as to lessen the distance of the sledge journey as far as possible, but at a point at which it can receive adequate medical and general supplies, e.g., railhead, town or village, or village connected up to railhead by good tracks.

To illustrate Casualties on the Battlefield (see text)

(B) STRAGGLERS fall under 2 headings:—

   (1) Those who can be carried on.

   (2) Those who must be evacuated at once.

(1) THOSE WHO CAN BE CARRIED ON and become effective in a short time require sledges for their transport and coverings to keep them warm. To be dealt with by the Mobile Column Medical Unit.

(2) CASES WHICH REQUIRE IMMEDIATE EVACUATION

Cases of accidental injury and sickness may require arrangements as elaborate and careful as those required for wounded men. The same system can be adopted.

NOTE:—

In the case of several Mobile Columns operating by different routes against the same objective, Relay Posts will be necessary on all routes until the objective is taken. When the objective is taken the Relay Posts on one route only need be retained (i.e., one with best surface and shortest). As soon as this is definitely established the others can be returned to the starting point.

CHAPTER VI.

ORGANISATION.

In considering the question as to how the Scheme of Evacuation should be carried out, as already stated (see "Scheme of Evacuation"), I decided to follow as far as possible the routine methods in practice in the army.

On mature consideration it seemed to me necessary that the work should as far as possible be carried out by one Unit of the R.A.M.C., because the ordinary R.A.M.C. training did not provide for the special nature of this work, and it would be necessary to train all ranks in the country itself.

In "Scheme of Evacuation" I have stated that there would be in connection with each Mobile Column two distinct Medical Units, i.e., the Mobile Column Medical Unit and the Relay System, and that the former should form an integral portion of the Mobile Column. The resources of the Mobile Columns, however, did not permit of the maintenance of a large number of spare Medical Officers and other ranks of the R.A.M.C., but in the case of wastage from sickness or casualty it would be necessary to replace them, and the training and supply of these reserves should devolve upon the R.A.M.C. Unit.

The Unit actually made responsible would depend upon the total number of Mobile Columns engaged, and the number likely to be engaged at any one time. In the Syren Force I decided that a Section of a Field Ambulance should be the responsible Unit, but for large numbers a complete Field Ambulance could be used.

The Section of the Field Ambulance, to be called the Mobile Section, would therefore function as follows:—

(1) Provide personnel and maintain the strength of the Mobile Column Medical Unit.

(2) Be entirely responsible for the Relay System, i.e., the Evacuation of Wounded for the Mobile Column Aid Post.'

(3) Act as a school of training in the methods of winter travel.

Should the personnel of the Section not be adequate for every possibility, personnel from other Units should be temporarily attached for a course of training, on the completion of which they should return to their own units, but be liable to be called upon in case of emergency.

As the work would almost certainly entail considerable hardship, I considered that all ranks engaged should be fit men, and, if possible volunteers. Some men find a pleasure in overcoming difficulties, and are, in troublesome situations, by their keenness and energy, able to perform better than men whose heart is not in their work. This view was strengthened by the experience of the winter's campaign.

On the above considerations I submitted the following to the A.D.M.S. Syren, and at the completion of the winter campaign I saw no reason to change it:—

1. The Unit responsible for the evacuation of wounded from Mobile Columns should be a Mobile Section of a Field Ambulance.
2. The personnel of this Section, both Officers and O.R.,1 should be composed of fit men.
3. The O.C.2 Mobile Section should, if possible, be experienced in the technique of travel in snowbound regions, and so be able to adapt his arrangements to the varying conditions under which Mobile Columns may operate.
4. The organisation of the Mobile Section should arrange for:—
    (a) Providing of M.O.'s and O.R. for Mobile Columns. These M.O.'s should be attached to parties where the number of men engaged warrants it; in the case of small parties a N.C.O. may be substituted.
    (b) Establishment of a system of evacuation.
5. For training purposes, the section should be mobilised at a centre as one Unit, and Officers and O.R. trained in all branches of Mobile Column work.
6. For active operations the organisation should be divided into two groups.
    (a) Mobile Column Medical Units.
    (b) Relay Systems.
   The number of these Units and systems for any one operation will vary with the number of separate parties used, and the conditions under which each is operating.
7. The Mobile Section should also act as a Training School for this special type of work. Officers and O.R. could thus be attached temporarily, pass through a course of instruction, and return to their own Units, and an adequate supply of trained personnel maintained.

THE MOBILE COLUMN'S MEDICAL UNIT.

1. The Mobile Column Medical Unit will consist nominally of 1 M O. and 4 O.R. R.A.M.C., who will be selected for each operation by the O.C. Section.
2. During the actual operation the M.O. will be under the command of the O.C. Mobile Column or Party, and hold a position similar to that of a Regimental Medical Officer. He will make, in conjunction with the O.C. Mobile Column or party, all necessary arrangements for the collection and conveyance of wounded from the fighting area to the Aid Post.
3. He will advise the O.C. Column as to the dangers of Frostbite, and arrange in conjunction with him for its prevention.
4. A scale of equipment for each Unit will be laid down, but the actual equipment carried will vary with circumstances at the discretion of the O.C. Mobile Section.

THE RELAY SYSTEM.

1. Each Relay System will be composed of a number of Relay Units, each self dependent, and capable of forming a Relay Post.
2. The Relay Unit will consist normally of 1 N.C.O. and 3 O.R., and this will be the organisation on which the Relay System depends. Each Unit will be self-contained, capable of expansion, and sufficiently mobile to enable it to accompany or follow up an advancing column to a selected position, and there function as a Relay Post.
3. The function of a Relay Post will vary according to circumstances. It may be merely a post where dressings are renewed, warm food given, and the wounded man passed on. It should, however, be capable of expansion into a Resuscitation post, where a severely wounded man can be detained and treated until fit to continue his journey.
4. The site of the Relay Post will vary with circumstances. Wherever possible it should be established in a clean and warm room, fitted with cooking arrangements. In unpopulated areas a tent may have to be used, and all cooking arrangements transported.
5. A scale of equipment will be laid down, but the actual equipment carried will vary with circumstances, at the discretion of the O.C. Mobile Section.

1 O.R.—Other Ranks.   2 O.C.—Officer Commanding.

CHAPTER VII.

EQUIPMENT

When an expedition leaves a centre of supply for a definite period, during which it is impossible to obtain any fresh supplies or to replace articles not effective, its success depends to a very large degree upon the completeness of preparation prior to setting out. How much this has been realised by explorers in ice-bound regions is evident in their records, in which almost unanimously a considerable part has been devoted to the organisation and equipment.

So in the case of the Mobile Columns. The amount of Equipment for dealing with casualties had to be rigidly limited owing to the great difficulty of transport, and only that carried which could be relied upon to safely reach its destination.

It was, therefore, of the utmost importance that the Medical Equipment should be selected with a view to the following properties:—
(1) Must be light and capable of being compactly disposed on the sledges.
(2) Must be effective, each article capable of functioning when actually put to use.
(3) Must consist of those things only which are necessary, and every unnecessary article eliminated.
(4) Must not be complicated, but simple and easy to use.

From the above considerations it is seen that much, and in many cases the lives of men, depended upon the Equipment. I deemed it necessary, therefore, in considering "The Evacuation of Wounded" as a whole, to pay careful attention to the equipment and enter carefully into every detail. I decided to lay down a definite establishment, to be rigidly maintained, for each Unit and Sub-Unit, based upon the conditions met with in Barren Areas. When I had worked out these establishments they were tested by making repeated short journeys, every article enumerated being used and put to the test under the actual conditions in which they would be required.

For descriptive purposes the Equipment is considered under the following headings:—
(1) Stretcher-bearers.
(2) The Regimental Aid Post.
(3) The Ambulance Sledges.
(4) The Relay Units.

From the diagrams it will be seen that every link in the system of Evacuation is covered. The Advanced Dressing Station, though of great importance from point of view of location, does not further enter into the Scheme of Evacuation.

DETAILS OF EQUIPMENT.

In considering the details of Equipment I had nothing to guide me except experience in polar regions and experimental journeys made in the country previous to operations.

In preparation they were arrived at by drawing upon the imagination, and, conceiving a mind picture of a wounded man, following him along his journey through the four links in the Evacuation mentioned above.

1. THE STRETCHER-BEARERS.

When wounded, the man is attended to on the spot by the Regimental Stretcher-bearers, who render first aid and convey him as rapidly as possible to the Regimental Aid Post. The equipment required for this part of the journey is as follows:—

For rendering First Aid (a):

> First field and shell dressings for applying to wound.
> Bandages, roller and triangular.
> Wool in compressed packets.

I decided that the Stretcher Bearers should travel as lightly as possible, and should therefore be taught to improvise splints and tourniquets from the abundant material* on the spot, to assist in which each Stretcher-bearer would be supplied with a heavy hunting knife.

For Transport to Aid Post (b):

> If possible use animals:—Sledges and animals suitable to the area (see Transport), each sledge to be fitted with a stretcher and sleeping bag (type for wounded)[1], which would be carried unfastened and could be rapidly thrown over the patient.

> If impossible to use animals (e.g., in circumstances where cover could be found for men but not for animals, or where animals would—owing to the noise of battle—get out of hand) man-haulage sledges[2] would be used, with man-harness for pulling by the Stretcher-bearers.

(a) Carried always by the Stretcher-bearer, renewable at the Aid Post.
(b) Transported by the Mobile Column Medical Unit and included in the list of equipment for same.
* The area of operations being densely covered with forest, trees and fallen branches abounded in all parts.

1, 2, Etc. See Chapter VIII.

2. THE REGIMENTAL AID POST.

The wounded man is attended to at the Aid Post by the Medical Officer and his personnel, wounds dressed, hot food given, sanitary requirements attended to. Finally he is prepared for the long sledge journey.

The equipment required at this stage is as follows:—

For the Aid Post, a tent[3] with waterproof floor cloth, to prevent wet from melted snow coming through, and fitted with a Beatrice Stove for maintaining a comfortable temperature. (This type of stove is quite adequate if the tent is wind proof.)

Medical equipment, including sterilising apparatus, instruments, dressings, splints, and drugs.

For cooking and serving food and providing hot water: Primus stove, kettle, camp kettle (lid acts as frying pan) and sauce-pan. Mugs, plates, knives, forks, spoons, and mess tins.

For sanitary needs of patient: Bed pan and urinal.

Food, fuel, medical comforts.

Camp accessories: Matches, candles, hurricane lamp, electric torch, axes, saw, shovel, rope.

For preparation for long journey:—Sleeping-bag (same as that used by Stretcher-bearers, in which patient is now disposed and bag clipped up all round—vide infra), blanket, hot water bottle[4], muff warmers, frost bite socks[5].

To prevent fouling of the bag by blood and other discharges, soak pads (large square pads of wool covered by gauze) to be placed under patient, jaconet (to cover bottom of bag).

3. THE AMBULANCE SLEDGE (a).

The patient is taken over from the Aid Post by the Relay System, and evacuated by sledge to the Advanced Dressing Station. The equipment necessary for this transport is as follows:—

For transport: Sledge and Animals suitable to the area of operations. (See Transport.)

For protection against cold: Sleeping-bag, blanket, hot water bottle, muff warmers, frost-bite socks. (It is unnecessary to change the patient from one sleeping-bag to the other, but to maintain the establishment of the Mobile Column Medical Unit it is necessary to carry the above articles as part of the equipment of the Ambulance Sledge, to be exchanged for those received.)

For providing hot drinks en route: Thermos flask and feeding-cup.

For sanitary requirements: A urine bottle and bed-pan.

Accessories: Axe, electric torch, matches.

First Aid Medical Supplies: First field dressings, bandages (roller and triangular), wool (compressed packets).

4 THE RELAY POST.

Here the Ambulance Sledge halts. The patient receives hot food, his wounds are redressed if necessary, his sanitary needs attended to. If necessary he is retained for resuscitation, but normally as soon as the above arrangements are completed he is passed on to the next Relay Post.

The necessary equipment for the Relay Post is:—
Tent and floorcloth (tent warmed by a Beatrice Stove).
Medical, cooking, and sanitary equipment and camp accessories as for Regimental Aid Post.
Spare, to replace damaged or lost articles: Sleeping-bags, blankets, hot water bottles, frost-bite socks.

(a) The Equipment of the Ambulance Sledge to be included in Relay System Equipment.

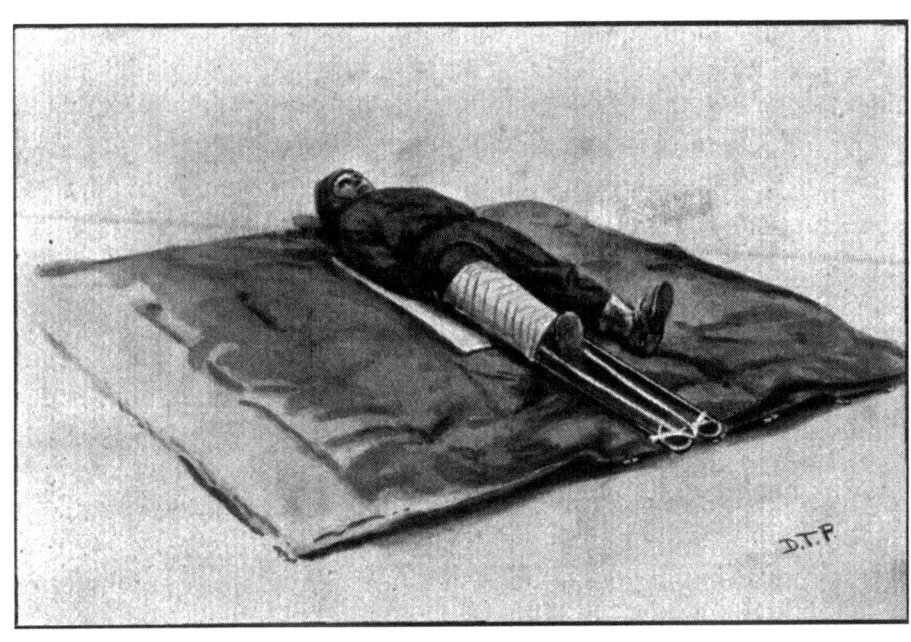

CHAPTER VIII.

SOME SPECIAL ARTICLES OF EQUIPMENT.

SLEEPING-BAG FOR WOUNDED.

In deciding upon the means to be adopted to protect the patient from cold, the following points were taken into consideration:—

(A)
(1) Material used must be capable of sufficient insulation.

(2) The shape must be such that the patient can be completely surrounded, and no openings be left permitting entry of cold air.

(3) Must allow sufficient ventilation, i.e., must be sufficiently porous to allow evaporation of perspiration. Water-proof covers cannot be used.*

(4) While meeting condition No. 3 must be wind-proof to prevent cold air passing through the texture.

(5) To meet general requirements of the Equipment, must be light and capable of being compactly disposed on the sledges.

(B) The final design must permit:

(1) Of exposing any one part of the body without uncovering the whole body.

(2) Of the application of splints, including Thomas splints for fractured femur.

(3) Of manipulation by fingers benumbed by intense cold.

(4) Of being easily cleaned and aired, since each bag would be used for a different man on each occasion.

* Personally observed on Italian Mountain Front, where troops were issued with sheepskin bags with waterproof covers. The perspiration passed through the bag, but was retained by the cover, and the bag when not in use froze stiff. Ablation could not take place. The bags eventually became saturated, and the men suffered severely from rheumatism. On removal of the covers these effects passed off.

The following bag is considered to most satisfactorily meet all the above conditions. (See illustration.)

MATERIAL.

Down contained in a quilt of mixed wool and cotton material, and covered by light, but strong, finely-woven cloth.

SHAPE.

Square, 7ft. by 7ft., fitted with toggles whereby the sides and bottom can be toggled up to form a bag, the toggles and eyes so disposed that when the bag is closed they form a double line down the front of the patient, making an overlap to exclude wind, and giving a double-breasted effect. At the foot they should be arranged so that when the toggles are secured there is one upward turn of the foot of the bag, thus rigidly excluding all cold air from the feet.

FASTENINGS.

Toggles of wood with eyes of whipcord are used in preference to metal clips and eyes, being poorer conductors of heat and more easy to manipulate with benumbed fingers.

METHOD OF DISPOSAL OF PATIENT.

(i) Without splints. The bag is laid flat and open. The patient is laid on it in the middle and flat on his back with legs straight out. The ends of the bag are brought round sufficiently to overlap in front and toggled. A turn upwards is taken at the bottom and the toggles secured. The patient is now completely insulated except at the neck, at which point it is difficult to completely exclude draughts of air. To obviate this a light blanket, to be disposed about the shoulders of the patient, is made part of the equipment, and in the Equipment the term "Sleeping-bag for Wounded" includes the light blanket.

(ii) With splints. The bag is made sufficiently roomy to include, without difficulty, all short splints. In the case of thigh splints, e.g., Liston and Thomas splints, the bag is laid flat over a stretcher, the patient laid on his back as before, and the splint applied. The bag is disposed as before, with the exception of the foot end. The splint protrudes through the open end, but the foot remains inside.

The toggles on either side of the splint are secured to the corresponding eyes, and any draught excluded by packing round with a blanket, an extra number of which for this purpose is included in the establishment.

The protruding portion of the splint can (in the case of a Liston) be placed in a slot, or (in the case of a Thomas) be secured to a suspension bar on the stretcher.

ATTENDANCE ON THE PATIENT WHILST IN THE SLEEPING BAG.

To attend to any one portion of the patient the necessary number of toggles over that portion are unfastened. The bag being made of flexible material permits of any one portion being pulled open whilst the rest remains undisturbed. To attend to the feet the foot end of the bag is opened up. A bed-pan or urinal can be passed in and the bag again closed till the article is ready to be removed.

THE MEDICAL TENT. (See Illustration).

The chief points in connection with the type of tent to be selected for medical purposes are as follows:—

(1) It should give the maximum accommodation in comparison with weight.

(2) An extended reconnaissance of the country showed that the area of operation was covered almost in its entirety with trees, many of which were long and slender and suitable for tent poles and pegs. The type of tent could therefore be selected independent of the weight of poles and pegs required.

(3 To enable an adequate temperature to be maintained inside by economical means it must be windproof.

The following design was selected:

MATERIAL.

Light, but closely woven canvas.

SHAPE.

Wigwam pattern, with ridge poles on supporting crossed poles at each end. The ground space was rectangular in shape and capable of accommodating (when otherwise empty) 11 stretchers. The side valances were 18 in. high, allowing ample height for inside work. Attached to the valances all round the base was a snow flap, which lay flat on the ground where the tent was pitched. With snow piled on this the bottom of the tent was absolutely draught proof. The entrance was of the folding over type, with double fastenings.

HOT WATER BOTTLE.

(4) The kind most suitable is that known in Army Equipment as a "Stomach Warmer." It is composed of a stoppered rubber hot water bottle covered by a jacket of flannel. It is better than a stone bottle in that, should the latter inadvertently be left unemptied, and exposed to cold, the water inside freezes and cracks the jar. In the case of the rubber bottle no harm results. It is also lighter and more easily packed.

FROST BITE SOCKS.

(5) These are composed of a mixture of wool and cotton, and are shaped like a boot, but are of considerably greater capacity, and are made to fasten down the front. In the case of frost-bite, or in the case of a man suffering from shock or collapse who is liable to frost-bite, the feet are wrapped loosely in cotton wool and lightly bandaged. A large pair of bed socks is pulled over the bandages. The frost-bite socks are filled loosely with hay or sennegrass (which must be dry) and fitted over the whole., The front is then laced tight to exclude entrance of cold air. It is essential when the whole is completed, that the socks fit loosely and the feet are in no way constricted.

CHAPTER IX.

FROST-BITE.

My experience of Polar Climates taught me that Frost-Bite was a condition very liable to supervene, even on healthy men, whilst living under the conditions as met with by the Mobile Columns.

The parts of the body most liable to frost-bite are the exposed parts of the face, the tips of the ears, the fingers, and the feet. In parts other than the feet the condition is usually not serious. Frost-bite of the face and ears if neglected may cause some disfigurement but no real crippling. Frost-bite of the hands can usually quickly be recognised, and easily treated by the simple and effective expedient of thrusting the hands inside the clothing next to the warm skin.

Frost-bite of the feet, however, is a serious condition fraught with great danger to the man so attacked; it may have far-reaching results and involve the need for amputation and consequent severe crippling.

Its onset is frequently insidious in that the feet may become frost-bitten without their owner being in the least aware anything is amiss. This happens even to the experienced, and can be combated only by constant watchfulness and periodical removal of the footgear for inspection of the toes.

Footgear in cold climate is elaborate, and requires for its removal that fingers be exposed, and in the process they are often frost-bitten. I found that troops frequently neglected to examine their feet; and it was probable that sick and wounded men would not trouble to do so at all.

I therefore considered that arrangements for the prevention and treatment of frost-bite of the toes should have an important place in the scheme of evacuation.

POINTS IN PREVENTION OF FROST-BITE.
AIR SPACE ROUND FEET.

(1) Experience and actual testing of many forms of footgear have shown that the best types are those which are loosely fitting and so have a non-conducting air space round the feet. Caeteris Paribus the feet will be warmer if three pairs of socks are worn than if two pairs only are worn, but if by adding the third pair the feet are constricted, this will not be the case. Footgear, however, if left too loose becomes unwieldy, and so for general use the air space so left must be very small. It is a practical point that cold feet at the end

of a march can be rendered more comfortable by removal of a pair of socks. Another practical point is that to prevent constriction socks must be worn in series, i.e., each additional pair must be a size larger than the one immediately inside it.

AVOIDANCE OF WET.

(2) Damp and wet predispose to frost-bite. There is always a certain amount of perspiration from the feet, and the footgear should be composed of materials which will not cause retention of moisture. Gum boots are useless for this reason. Material which allows moisture to pass out also permits damp to pass in. In extreme cold the snow is quite dry, but small quantities settling on the tops of the boots are melted by the warmth of the feet, and in this way the socks may at times become wet.

In nearly every case Casualties were admitted to the Regimental Aid Post with feet wet from this cause. This can be counteracted by supplying dry socks in graduated sizes.

EFFECTIVE INSULATION ON THE SLEDGE JOURNEY.

(3) This has been dealt with under "Sleeping Bag for Wounded," the chief essential being to prevent cold draughts of air passing through the flaps of the bag to the feet.

NOTES ON THE USE OF OIL AND GREASE.

Whale oil was extensively used in the British Army during the late war for protection of the feet against cold.

Instructions were given that it was to be rubbed into the feet until the oil disappeared.

Camphor grease was used in the same way by the Italian Army.

It is a matter of common belief, shared by many medical men, that all oils and grease are poor conductors of heat.

During a visit to the Whaling Station of S. Georgia, where whale oil abounded, I made a practice of rubbing the oil into my boots, with the object of making them warmer and more waterproof. I discovered that the oil had the opposite effect. The whalers informed me that this was a matter of common experience amongst them, and that they made a practice of removing as much whale oil as possible from their boots each night.

Whilst serving as Surgeon to the Imperial Trans-Antarctic Expedition it was my duty to flense and cut up seals. In the process my left hand grasped the seal and became well anointed with blubber oil. My right hand held the flensing knife and was not so anointed. Following the operation I wiped my hands with snow (which did not completely remove the grease), dried off surplus moisture, and replaced them in mitts.

On the return journcy to camp my left hand always felt much colder than the right.

In the later stages of the same expedition, loss of all stores compelled members of the Expedition to wear their clothing without change for eleven months. Parts of them became very greasy, and it was found that these parts conducted the cold more readily than clothing which was not greasy.

Socks which had been worn for some time and become slightly greasy were less warm than clean dry socks.

A type of sock is manufactured by certain firms known as the "Arctic sock," and is recommended for use in Switzerland and other cold countries. They are composed of thick wool imbued with grease. They were tested by numbers of the Expedition and found to be less warm than ungreased socks.

Whilst serving on the Italian Mountain Front as a Regimental Medical Officer, it became necessray to take stringent measures to prevent frost-bite. Whale oil was issued, with instructions that it should be rubbed into the feet twice daily. I carried out the following experiments:—

(1) I rubbed oil briskly into my left foot and gave my right foot a brisk dry rub night and morning. I found that my right foot was the more comfortable. The difference was, however, not marked, and might be due to bias.

(2) I instructed the Regimental Stretcher-bearers to pick out a certain number of men and rub with oil one foot only. The replies were conflicting, and many men were unable to distinguish between the two feet.

(3) I then issued orders that one foot was to be rubbed with oil and the other dry rubbed by another Stretcher-bearer whose hands were not oily. The replies were almost unanimously in favour of the dry rubbing.

(4) I acquired some clean, dry socks, and arranged for one of these to be worn on the dry-rubbed foot, and a dried, used (and therefore slightly greasy) sock to be worn on the foot rubbed with oil. Men so tested stated unanimously that the dry-rubbed foot with the clean sock remained much warmer than the other.

The same experiments were carried out with camphor grease obtained from an Italian Medical Officer. I found that the camphor grease produced a greater temporary local reaction than whale oil, but in other respects the results were similar.

CONCLUSION.

(1) Troops are so careless that often they do not remove their socks for several days on end unless compelled to do so by disciplinary measures. Foot-drill, with the use of whale oil, compels that the boots and socks be removed twice daily, and rubbing the oil into the feet ensures that the feet are vigorously massaged. Consequently the use of whale oil and camphor grease has in this way had beneficial effects.

(2) That brisk, dry rubbing without oil produces better results than massage with oil.

(3) That steps should be taken to prevent access of grease or oil to the skin or clothing.

The following arrangements were made for

PREVENTION OF FROST-BITE OF SICK & WOUNDED:

Where the exigencies of the situation permitted of it, all men's toes were examined at the Regimental Aid Post.

The feet received a brisk, dry rub.

If the socks were wet they were replaced by clean, dry pairs.

The footgear was replaced, with one pair of socks less than worn ordinarily, thus permitting a larger air space.

In lying cases, i.e., those who during the journey would not be able at any time to walk, the outer coverings (boots or mocassins) were not replaced, because it was found by experience that the feet remained warmer without them, provided that there was sufficient protection from wind and draughts.

TREATMENT OF THOSE ALREADY FROST-BITTEN,

and also for cases of severe shock and collapse:—

The feet are loosely wrapped in cotton wool, thoroughly dried at a Primus stove, and which is applied slightly warm (not hot). Frost-bite socks are then applied. (See Equipment—Frost-bite Socks.)

All cases are then placed in the special sleeping-bag for wounded, and air leaks carefully shut off. In case of fracture of the lower limb in which a splint protrudes from the foot of the bag this precaution is particularly necessary.

When possible, hay is packed loosely round, with special attention to the foot end of the bag.

CHAPTER X.

CONCLUSION.

The general arrangement, as set out, when put into practice proved satisfactory. Sick and wounded were, in every case, rapidly evacuated, and arrived at the Advanced Dressing Station in good condition. The Equipment, as laid down, small though it appears to be, was quite adequate.

Anti-Frost-bite measures were successful; in no case did frost-bite occur during the evacuation.

All ranks stated that they were comfortable on the journey. Many complained of great discomfort from using a bed-pan whilst in the sledge, owing to its extreme cold. I saw no effective way of overcoming this without greatly increasing the weight and bulk of the sledge load.

The following points, which were noted during the winter, are of interest:—

(1) The number of men wounded in any engagement in no case exceeded 15% of the number engaged.

(2) The number of sick averaged twice to three times the number of wounded.

(3) The cases of sickness, with a few exceptions, fell under two headings:—

(a) EXHAUSTION.

This manifested itself in two ways:—

(i.) PYREXIAL TYPE.

These cases usually occurred after a spell of prolonged exertion, and were seen on the morning following an action. The temperature varied from 100° to 104° F., the pulse was full and bounding, and the symptoms were those associated with pyrexia. The fever lasted from two to eight days, complete recovery following with rest in bed. This type was frequently seen.

(ii.) A-PYREXIAL TYPE.

This type was not so common, and was seen only amongst Serbian* troops, always after very great exertion. It was generally reported that they could not be roused, and when seen were found to be drowsy, lethargic, pale, and cold. The temperature was subnormal, and the pulse weak

and rapid. The pupils were, in many cases, dilated, and in a few cases, unequal in size; in no case was there any evidence of injury. The state of collapse was, in some cases, so marked that no response could be obtained, and the patients had to be lifted with the special bags and carried on stretchers to the sledge. I lost trace of these cases after evacuation.

* The Serbian Troops consisted of a body of picked men, and on occasion the operations carried out by them entailed much greater exertion than that required by the other Allied Troops.

(b) FROST-BITE.

The number of these cases was low, and they were due to failure to comply with instructions.

The Shackleton pattern boots and graduated series of socks which were supplied to troops, proved absolutely efficient for the protection of the feet. The onset was due to wearing boots or mocassins so tight that the feet were constricted. Treatment was effective, and carried out on the lines already indicated. In only two cases did gangrene set in, and in them the onset occurred under most exceptional circumstances.

(4) Some cases of shell shock were seen amongst Russian troops. The amount of shell fire was almost negligible. The cause was apparently excitement following on fatigue.

APPENDICES.

APPENDIX I. i. Establishment of One Mobile Column Medical Unit.
   a. Reindeer Transport.
   b. Horse Transport.
 ii. Establishment of One Relay Post.

APPENDIX II. i. Equipment of One Mobile Column Medical Unit.
 ii. Equipment of Relay System.
   a. Relay Post.
   b. Ambulance Sledge.

EQUIPMENT OF MOBILE COLUMN MEDICAL UNIT.

MEDICAL.
Medical Companion	1
Steriliser	1
Rolls, Instruments	1
Forceps, Tooth, roll	1

DRESSINGS.
Wool .... lbs.	10
Lint .... ,,	1
Gauze (compressed) ...yds.	20
Jaconet .... ,,	1
Adhesive plaster ...1in. rolls	12
Bandages, roller	50
,, triangular	50

SPLINTS.
Gooch .... rolls	2
Thomas'	2
Zinc perforated strips	6
Flannel .... yds.	3
Adhesive plaster, broad rolls	2
Tourniquets, rubber	2
Shell Dressings	20

BRITISH RED CROSS SOCIETY SUPPLY.
Shell Dressings	12
Thermos flasks	2
Sleeping socks ...... pairs	20
Frost-bite socks	6

R.A.O.C. SUPPLIES.
Sledges (Antarctic) ...... 11ft.	1
,, ,, ...15ft.	10
,, Russian pattern	*3
Tents, Mob. Col'n Patt. ...large	2
,, ,, ,, ...small	1
Floorcloths for tents ......large	2
,, ,, ...small	1
Bags, Sleeping, Mob. Col'n patt.	5
Bags, Sleeping, for wounded	20
Clothing, Mob. Col. scale, sets complete	5
Stretchers	10

Blankets	25
Stomach Warmers	20
First field dressings	50
Camp kettles	2
Saucepans	2
Axes, Canadian	2
,, light hand	1
Saws, hand ripping	1
Shovels	2
Lamps, hurricane	2
Stove, Primus	1
Torches, electric	2
Kettles	1
Tin Shears	1
Petrol tins .... 2 gal. size	1
Cups, feeding	2
Urine Bottle	1
Bedpan	1
Stove, Beatrice	1
Mugs, pint, enamel	10
Plates, enamel	10
Knives	10
Forks	10
Spoons	12
Mess tins	2
Rope, lashing coils	½
Knives, hunting, 6in.	5
Harness, sets	5

* This number allows for carrying of equipment only. Local supplies will be used for evacuation of wounded.

R.A.S.C. SUPPLIES.
Paraffin .... galls	2
Spirits, Methylated ......pints	½
Candles .... lbs.	5
Brandy .... bot.	1
Oxo .... lbs.	2
Milk .... tins	10
Tea .... lbs.	2
Sugar .... lbs.	4

EQUIPMENT OF RELAY POST.

MEDICAL.
Medical Companion 1

DRESSINGS.
Wool ....lbs. 12
Lint .... ,, 1
Gauze ....yds. 30
Jaconet .... ,, 1
Adhesive plaster ....1in. rolls 12
Bandages, roller 50
 ,, triangular 12
Shell dressings 12
Tourniquets 1

SPLINTS.
Gooch 2
Thomas' 2
Zinc, perforated strips 6
Flannel ....yds. 3
Adhesive plaster, broad rolls ... 2

BRITISH RED CROSS SOCIETY SUPPLIES.
Shell dressings 12
Muff warmers 40
Sleeping Socks ....pairs 12
Frost-bite socks .... ,, 2
Thermos flasks 1

R.A.O.C. SUPPLIES.
Sledges, Antarctic 11ft. 1
 ,, Russian pattern 2
Tent, Barbateau pattern 2
Floorcloth for same 1
Bags, sleeping, Mobile Col. patt. 4
Clothing, Mobile Column scale... 4
Bags, sleeping, wounded 2
Stretchers 2
Blankets 10

RELAY SYSTEM.
Stomach warmers 2
First field dressings 25
Camp kettles 2
Axes, Canadian 2
Saws, hand ripping 1
Shovels 2
Lamps, hurricane 2
Stove, Primus 1
Torches, electric 2
Kettle 1
Tin shears 1
Petrol Tin ....2 gal size 1
Cups, feeding 2
Bottle, urine 1
Bedpan 1
Stove, Beatrice 1
Saucepans 2
Mugs, pint, enamel 10
Plates, enamel 10
Knives 10
Forks 10
Spoons 12
Mess tins 2
Rope, lashing coils .... $\frac{1}{4}$
Knives, hunting 6in.. 4
Harness, Man-sets 4
Axes, light hand 1

R.A.S.C. SUPPLIES.
Paraffin ....galls. 2
Spirits, Methylated ....pints $\frac{1}{2}$
Candles ....lbs. 5
Brandy ....bot. 1
Oxo ....lbs. 1
Milk ....tins 6
Tea ....lbs. 2
Sugar .... lbs 6

EQUIPMENT OF AMBULANCE SLEDGE.

Jaconet ....yds. sq. 1
Soap pads 12
Bandages 3in. 12

BRITISH RED CROSS SOCIETY SUPPLIES.
Thermos flask 1
Muff warmers 2

Frost-bite socks 2
Bags, sleeping, for wounded 2
Cup, feeding 1
Urine bottle 1
Stomach warmers 2
Electric torch 1
First field dressings ,............... 6
Axe, light hand 1

ESTABLISHMENT.

ONE MOBILE COLUMN MEDICAL UNIT WITH HORSE TRANSPORT.

	Personnel					Sldg's Tents									Equipment, &c.									
	Officers	Sergeants	Corporals	Privates	Total	Antarctic	Ambulance	Large	Small	Sleeping Bags	Mess Tins & Spoons	Matches	Dixies	Candles LBS	Axes	Saws	Shovels	Special Rations LBS	Medical Gear LBS	Lamps	Primus	Oil GALS	Horses	Fodder
One Unit	1	...	...	6	7	1	...	2	1	7	7	7	2	2	2	1	2	175	100	1	1	2	1	140
Extras	...	...	...	...	...	...	10	...	...	20	...	...	...	...	1	...	...	...	...	...	...	...	10	1400
Total	1	...	...	6	7	1	10	2	1	27	7	7	2	2	3	1	2	175	100	1	1	2	11	1540
A. S. C.	...	...	...	11	11	†	...	††	...	**	11	11	2	2	2	1	...	275	...	1	...	...	‖	140
Complete "Horse-drawn" Unit	1	...	...	17	18	2	10	3	1	38	18	18	4	4	5	2	4	450	100	2	1	2	12	1680

* 4 R.A.M.C. orderlies, 12 A.S.C. or Russian drivers, 1 A.S.C. Tent man.
† 1 sledge for unit gear, 1 for A.S.C. drivers' gear.
‡ 1 for Aid Post.
** 20 bags for wounded.
‖ 2 for †, 10 for ambulance sledges.

ESTABLISHMENT.

ONE MOBILE COLUMN MEDICAL UNIT with REINDEER TRANSPORT.

	Personnel					Sldg's		Tents		Equipment, &c.													Horses	Fodder	Reindeer
	Officers	Sergeants	Corporals	Privates	Total	Antarctic	Ambulance	Large	Small	Sleeping Bags	Mess Tins & Spoons	Matches (BXS)	Dixies	Candles	Axes	Saws	Shovels	Special Rations (LBS)	Medical Gear (LBS)	Lamps	Primus	Oil (GALS)	Horses	Fodder	Reindeer
One Unit	1	...	...	6	7	1	...	2	1	7	7	7	2	2	2	1	2	175	100	1	1	2	1	...	...
Extras	...	...	...	*	...	...	10	...	...	20 ††	10 §	10	2 ‖	...	...	...	...	250 ¶	...	...	...	...	...	140	20 **
Total	1	...	...	6	7	1	10	2	1	27	17	17	4	2	2	1	2	425	100	1	1	2	1	140	20

* 4 R.A.M.C. orderlies, 2 A.S.C. drivers.
† 1 sledge for gear.
‡ 10 sledges for wounded.
§ 7 for unit personnel, 10 for Lapp drivers of ‡‡
‖ 2 for unit personnel, 2 for Lapp drivers of ‡‡
¶ 175 lbs. for unit. 250 lbs. for Lapps.
** 10 to draw, 10 to break trail.
†† 20 special bags for wounded.

ESTABLISHMENT.

ONE RELAY UNIT—Self-contained for 10 days.

Personnel				Equipment, Sledging													Equipment—Medical.								
Officers	N.C.O.s	Privates	Total	Sledge	Tent	Sleeping Bags	Dixies	Axes, Canadian	Saws	Shovels	Mess Tins & Spoons	Matches	Candles	Special Rations	Lamp, Hurricane	Primus Stove	Beatrice Stove	Oil	Kettles	Cups, Feeding	Urine Bottles	Bed Pans	Torch, Electric	Blankets	E.F. Dressings	Medical	Med. Comforts
												BXS LBS	BXS LBS	SUT LBS				GALS							TNS LBS	TNS LBS	TNS LBS
...	1	3	4	1	1	4	2	2	1	2	4	4 4	4 4	4 160	1	1	1	2	1	2	1	1	1	1 10	20	75	35

www.ingramcontent.com/pod-product-compliance
Lightning Source LLC
Chambersburg PA
CBHW080609090426
42735CB00017B/3377